be the CEO of your inner m;onkey

ULLAS DAS

QUANAH PARKER
QUANAH PARKER - AN IMPRINT BY
www.24by7publishing.com

This book, be the CEO of your Inner Monkey,
is written and self-published by Ullas Das.

Imprint: Quanah Parker - an imprint of 24by7Publishing.com

All the printing & distribution magic behind this book
is powered by:

24by7 Publishing
13 New Road, Kolkata - 51, India
www.24by7Publishing.com
mail@24by7publishing.com
+91 9831 470 133 / +91 9433 444 334

Any resemblance to real monkeys, living or extinct, is purely intentional.

Price: USD $14.99
INR ₹ 499.00

First Published in December, 2025
Version 1.00
ISBN: 978-81-994575-8-4

Powered by
24by7Publishing.com

m; dedication

Yes, my emotions are personal

To **Aurique** and **Aurhaan**,
who accidentally became the first CEOs in this book
by founding MONKE Inc. in a notebook
while their Papa was still working overtime
as a confused employee of his own mind.

You proved, with pencil and pure innocence,
that sometimes children remember
what adults have spent a lifetime forgetting.

m; read this first

How to Use This Book

Without Fighting Yourself

Be honest.
You didn't pick up this book because you love discipline.
You picked it up because something inside you is tired of failing at being the one in control.

This book is not a makeover manual.
It's a peace treaty between you and the noisy creature in your head
I call your **inner monkey**.

You know that part very well:

- The one that wants one more reel, one more snack, one more scroll.
- The one that panics when you open your to-do list.
- The one that promises, "From tomorrow I'll be perfect," and then disappears the moment tomorrow actually arrives.

Most productivity books secretly talk to you
as if you are a small, broken machine.

This book talks to you as if you are a human being who accidentally hired a very emotional, very powerful,
very easily-bored monkey as their CEO.

What this book will help you do

By the time you finish this book, you will:

- **Understand** why your inner monkey behaves the way it does
(and why discipline alone keeps failing).
- **Stop hating** yourself for not being "consistent enough".
- **Learn to negotiate** with your monkey instead of declaring war on it.
- **Build a simple, monkey-friendly routine** that you can actually live with on a normal, messy day.

No perfection, no 4am miracles.
Just a working relationship between you and your mind.

How to read this book (even with a short attention span)

You do **not** have to read this like a textbook.
In fact, your monkey will riot if you try.

Here's a gentler plan:

Start at the beginning
Let Chapters 1-4 introduce your monkey properly - where it came from, what it wants, and how an 11-year-old accidentally became CEO before most adults do.

Look for the m; icons
Whenever you see **m;** in this book, it simply means: "*Monkey-approved, pay attention.*"

There are two main kinds of monkey marks:

- **m; notes** - short, sharp ideas your monkey can understand at a glance.
  These are your "screenshot and save" lines.
- **m; activities** - tiny experiments.
  Not homework. Not punishment.
  Just small, curious tests you run
  with your monkey, not against it.

Don't wait for a perfect week
Start using ideas while your life is still messy: between school runs, during office stress, on days when you're too tired to impress anyone.

Try the Night Meeting at least once
In the second half of the book you'll meet my favourite ritual:

a quiet **night meeting** between you and your monkey.
One conversation, on one night,
can change how the next morning feels.

You don't have to turn your life upside down.
You just have to stop treating your monkey
like an enemy soldier
and start treating it like a confused, over-energised junior partner.

m; how a kid became ceo

A Short Backstory

This book did not start in a boardroom.
It started on a bed.

One evening, my twin boys, Aurique and Aurhaan,
were sprawled on the bed with a notebook.
I thought they were doodling.
They were not.

They were quietly building a company.

They drew boxes and arrows,
gave it a name - MONKE Inc. -
and started assigning roles:

- Who takes decisions.
- Who gets which bananas.
- Which monkey is allowed to press which button.

They were not thinking about psychology,
productivity,
or self-help categories on Amazon.
They were just doing what kids do best -
turning chaos into a game.

I watched them build MONKE Inc. on paper
with more clarity than many adults use
to build their actual lives.

Somewhere between their scribbles,
something clicked in my tired, adult brain:

> "What if my own mind also runs like a company?
> What if the problem is not that I'm lazy,
> but that I let the wrong monkey sit in the CEO chair?"

That question refused to leave.

This book is my attempt
to answer that question honestly
- as a parent, as a professional,
and as a human who has failed
every serious-looking productivity system
more times than I can count.

If you've ever felt like your mind is a noisy office
full of emotional employees and unfinished work,
you are in the right book.

Welcome to MONKE Inc.
It's time to meet your CEO.

m; the m;onkey map

1 - the m;onkey you didn’t know you had

Picture this.

It's 11:47 p.m.
Your phone is sitting on your chest like a small, glowing brick of guilt.

You've had a whole day to do The Important Thing.
The project.
The workout.
The call.
The "new life from today" plan.

Instead, your inner voice plays its greatest hits:

"I know exactly what to do... I just didn't do it."

"I'll start tomorrow."

"Just five more minutes."

"Let me scroll one last video."

"Today was not my day."

"I don't know why I wasted so much time."

And, on the quieter nights:

"Why am I like this?"

If any of those lines feel a little too familiar, I have good news and bad news.

Bad news: that voice is not going away on its own. Good news: it's not proof that you're broken. It's just... your monkey.

You've already met it.
You meet it every time you know exactly what to do and somehow don't do it.
Every time "morning-you" becomes a visionary and "night-you" becomes a negotiator.
Every time you promise "future-you" will be "a different person on Monday," as if a software update is secretly scheduled for Sunday midnight.

From the outside, this looks like laziness or lack of discipline.
From the inside, it feels like living with two people at once:

- one who wants to grow, build, create, change
- and one who just wants a little more comfort, a little less pressure, and five more minutes

This book is about the second one.
The jumpy one.
The dramatic one.
The one who panics when you open Excel and relaxes when you open YouTube.

That one is your monkey.

The monkey is the part of you that reacts before you think.
The part that fears change.
The part that loves comfort, hates boredom, and negotiates with your brain like a lawyer defending a professional slacker.

And for years, you believed this monkey was you.

Before I show you otherwise, let me ask you something honestly.

How many times have you worn a mask?

Not the Halloween kind.
A social mask.

At a job interview.
At an office meeting.
At a wedding, a school event, a family dinner, even while posting "candid" photos on social media.

That perfectly ironed **"I'm doing great"** face.
That controlled smile.
That polite, reasonable, LinkedIn-friendly version of you.

Meanwhile, inside your head, your monkey is bouncing around:

"Do I look stupid?"

"What if I say the wrong thing?"

"Please don't ask me anything."

"Why am I sweating?"

"I hope no one sees the real me."

"Can I leave now?"

On the outside, the mask is doing its job.
On the inside, the monkey is hanging from the ceiling fan, screaming.

You hide the monkey from the world.
You hide the monkey from your friends.
Eventually, you start hiding the monkey from yourself.

And yes - sometimes the mask helps you survive a situation.
No one wants to see your full emotional operating system during a performance review.

But here is the problem:

m; note

When you hide the monkey too long,
you start believing the mask is you.

And when that happens, the monkey doesn't disappear. It just gets... caged.

Caging the monkey doesn't make you mature.
It makes you tired.
It makes you anxious.
It makes you feel oddly disconnected from your own life.

You create routines that look good on paper and collapse in real life.
Plans that start out heroic and die by day three.
Ambitions that burn bright in your notebook and quietly burn you out in practice.

Not because you're weak.
Because the monkey has no space to breathe.

And this entire time, you blamed yourself.

Here is the truth that can change your life:

m; note
You are not the monkey.
You are the CEO of the monkey.

The moment you separate yourself from your impulses, you gain power.
The moment you see the monkey as a separate emotional creature inside you, you stop taking its reactions personally.

When the monkey panics, it doesn't mean *you* are a failure.

It means a scared part of you is trying to keep things familiar.

And the moment you start **leading** it - not fighting it - you unlock a different level of calm, consistency, and clarity.

Because if you are the CEO, then:

- The monkey's fear is feedback, not a verdict.
- The monkey's cravings are signals, not orders.
- The monkey's "I don't wanna" is the start of a negotiation, not the end of the story.

You've spent years either obeying the monkey or trying to beat it into silence.
Neither works for long.

This book is about a third option:
learning to sit down with the monkey like a slightly dramatic employee, listen to it, include it, and then guide it.

You don't fix your life by declaring war on your own brain.
You fix it by finally understanding the creature that's been running most of your decisions in the background.

Let me show you how it all began.

2 - why your m;onkey behaves this way: the science you were never told

Before we go any further, I want to tell you something nobody bothered to explain in school.

You are not designed for modern life.
Your brain architecture is millions of years old.
Your lifestyle is only a few decades old.

That's like asking a dinosaur to file taxes on an iPad.

We keep calling ourselves "lazy," "weak," "unmotivated," when in reality we're mostly running Stone Age software in a Silicon Valley world.

Let me put it in one sentence:

m; note

Your monkey brain is ancient.
Your world is brand new.

Your monkey was built for jungles, not offices.

For danger, not deadlines.

For threats, not unread emails.

For short bursts of activity, not 8-hour Zoom marathons.

For survival, not self-improvement.

For tribe approval, not LinkedIn endorsements.

Once you see this mismatch, a lot of your "problems" start looking a lot less personal and a lot more... biological.

Let's walk through what your monkey is actually trying to do all day.

Your monkey hates wasting fuel

Once upon a time (meaning: most of human history), calories were rare.

Your ancestors didn't have food delivery apps, "all you can eat" buffets, or midnight snacks. If they wanted to eat, they had to hunt, gather, climb, carry, chase, run, dig, and die (in some cases). Everything cost fuel - even in the last case.

So the monkey brain learned one simple rule:

"Don't waste energy unless you really have to."

Effort was risky. Effort meant burning calories. Burning calories meant less backup for the next emergency.

Fast forward to you, sitting on your couch, watching a 12-minute video essay about productivity... and somehow being too tired to wash three plates in the sink.

Starting a new routine feels exhausting.
Reading a book makes your eyes heavy after three pages.
A tiny chore like replying to one email feels strangely dramatic.
Planning your week feels like you've already worked a full shift.

Your monkey isn't lazy.
It's energy-efficient.

Every time you say, "Ugh, I'll do it later," a small ancient voice is whispering in the background: "*Save fuel. We might need it if something jumps at us.*"

Nothing is going to jump at you from behind the fridge, but the monkey doesn't know that. From its perspective, you're still one bad week away from the food running out.

Why "boring" feels secretly dangerous

Here's another weird thing.

In the wild, boredom was not a cute aesthetic. Boredom meant your alertness was dropping. Low alertness meant you were easier to catch, bite, and eat.

So the monkey built another rule:

"If things get too slow or repetitive, **wake up**. Something might be wrong."

That's why you can watch a three-hour movie but struggle to sit with a spreadsheet for ten minutes.

That's why cleaning a room feels painful, finishing a slow project feels like punishment, and long routines feel like mild torture.

Your nervous system is scanning for movement, change, noise, threat, opportunity. A sink full of dishes does not qualify. Your brain treats it like visual wallpaper, and your monkey quietly wanders off in search of something more interesting - usually your phone.

From your point of view: "*Why can't I just finish this stupid thing?*"
From the monkey's point of view: "*If I zone out here, we might miss a lion. Or a snack. Or a friend. Or anything that isn't this.*"

Your monkey is wired for shiny, not steady

In the jungle, **novelty** meant information.

New sound? New smell? New pattern in the bushes? That could be food, threat, weather, new tribe, new anything.

So the monkey got rewarded - literally with dopamine - for noticing what's new. The more new things it spotted, the more likely it was to survive.

Now put that same brain in front of 12 streaming platforms, 20 apps, infinite scroll, messages, notifications, pop-ups, reels, shorts, stories.

Your monkey is in Las Vegas.

Of course you start ten projects and finish none.
Of course the first day of a new goal feels magical, and day three feels like chewing cardboard.
Of course a new app, new notebook, new course feels way more exciting than continuing the old one.

You call it "I have zero consistency."
The monkey calls it **"business as usual."**

It's not morally inconsistent. It's just wired to chase newness - new hobbies, new ideas, new channels, new projects, new plans.

In the jungle, new information simply means survival advantage.

The jungle rewarded that. Your calendar doesn't.

Your monkey isn't inconsistent.
It's wired to chase newness.

Tell the Difference Between a Tiger and an Email

Emotions didn't evolve to be poetic. They evolved to keep you alive.

Fear, shame, embarrassment, anxiety, tension - these are all ways your system shouts:

"Something here might hurt us. Pay attention."

In the jungle, that made sense.
Rustling in the dark? Adrenaline.
Someone shouting? Adrenaline.
Strange shadow near the cave? Adrenaline.

Today, the shadows look different:

A small email from your manager feels like a tiny panic. Clients' meetings without a detailed agenda or generic subject feel like threats. Your to-do list feels like a wall. Even a simple social event where you don't know half the people can make the monkey go hyper-alert.

Your monkey doesn't understand the context. It only understands **"possible threat."**

The monkey brain doesn't know the difference between:

"This lion will kill me,"
and
"This deadline will embarrass me."

Same alarm system.
Wrong era.

So your body responds.

Your heart rate sneaks up as you open the inbox. You suddenly feel exhausted when you sit down for

that "important task."
You find yourself avoiding a conversation as if the person is literally carrying a spear.

From outside, it looks like procrastination.
From inside, it feels like staying alive.

What is your monkey's sacred word?

If you listen closely, your monkey really has only one prayer in life:

"Please... let it be comfortable."

In monkey-logic, comfort is not a luxury. Comfort is safety. Safety is survival.
Anything that feels sharp, exposed, effortful, or uncertain goes straight into the "maybe we die" folder.

Think about your laziest evenings.

You tell yourself you'll get up from the couch in two minutes.
You don't.
You promise you'll stop scrolling after this reel.
You don't.
You know you're not hungry, but your hand is in the snack packet again, simple survival mode.

From the outside, it looks ridiculous.
From the inside, the monkey is running a very old script:

- The couch feels like a cave.
- The blanket feels like fur.
- The glowing screen feels like a fire that keeps the dark away.
- Noise in the background feels like "the tribe is here, I'm not alone."

Out there - in the inbox, in the calendar, in the unfinished project - things bite:
judgment, expectations, deadlines, human eyes.

So the monkey does what it believes a loyal bodyguard should do: it keeps you small, soft, and still.

Skip the event. Stay home. Don't speak. Don't risk. Don't move.

When you hesitate before a call, when you freeze before starting, when you overreact to a small task and suddenly feel "too tired"... that's not random weakness. That's your monkey dragging you gently back toward the nearest safe, padded, familiar corner.

It's not trying to ruin your future.
It genuinely believes:

"If we stay quiet, low, and comfortable, nothing truly bad can happen to us."

Under almost every dramatic "I can't," there is the same quiet movement:
your monkey reaching for comfort like a scared child reaching for a blanket.

Meet your Executive Brain

Now let's talk about the other character in this story.

The rational, planning, logical part of your mind - the one that writes goals, makes spreadsheets, and says things like "From Monday I'll become serious" - that's the CEO.

In brain terms, this is your prefrontal cortex, the "thinking" brain.

It is... very young.

The monkey has millions of years of field experience. The CEO has maybe 40-50 thousand, and personally maybe 30-40 years at best.

Guess who wins most inner battles?

The ancient one.

Think of the monkey as your emotional operating system - the old, stubborn, always-on layer. The "CEO you" is basically an app installed on top.

Apps crash all the time. Operating systems just keep humming in the background.

That's why you can understand something perfectly and still not do it.

Your CEO is reading this book.

Your monkey didn't care about the CEO attending the training.

So What Does This Mean for You?

So what does all this science-without-the-labcoat mean for you?

It means you weren't a failure.
You weren't broken.
You weren't "not serious enough" or "too weak."

You were simply using a Stone Age brain to navigate a notification-addicted, always-online, productivity-obsessed world... and nobody gave you a user manual.

Your monkey has never understood modern life.
And nobody taught you how to lead it.

Until now.

In the next chapter, I'll tell you how this entire philosophy was born - not in a lab, not in a therapy room, and not in a productivity workshop.

It began the night I became a father.

A night when I realized:

I don't have just two babies.
I have three.
The third one lives inside me.

Let me take you there.

3 - the night i became a father... and a m;onkey ceo

I still remember the night the doctor said:

"You're having twins."

My wife and I just stared at each other - half-laughing, half-terrified, completely unprepared.

What made the moment heavier was the truth we were silently carrying:
life had already shaken us by the shoulder.

We had started our journey in Framingham, Massachusetts, young and hopeful, believing that hard work and talent would keep us safe in a foreign country.

But the day my wife conceived the twins,
I also lost a project.

And with that loss came a lesson nobody teaches you about the immigrant life:

m; note

You don't just lose a project.
You lose stability.
You lose sleep.
You lose your version of "tomorrow."

We moved soon after to Madison, Wisconsin -
in the dead heart of winter.

The interviewer warned me about the cold.
I shrugged.
In my arrogance I said,
"We survived minus ten in Boston - minus twenty will be the same."

It wasn't.

Cold like that is not a temperature.

It's a personality.

A presence.

It follows you everywhere.

Contractors had no covered parking.
So every morning before sunrise,
I stood in an open parking lot,
scraping ice with fingers turning numb,
cleaning the car just to drive to work.

Then I cleaned it again to bring my pregnant wife to her medical checkups.
Then again to return.
Then again after helping her up the stairs.

I cleaned the car more times per day
than I cleaned my thoughts.

And somewhere between the snow,
the fear,

the responsibility,
and the silent prayers I whispered during those drives,
a realization struck me:

m; note

"My monkey is terrified.
But I have to lead it anyway."

In that brutal winter,
while holding my wife's hand
and protecting two unborn babies,
I met the rawest version of myself -
a man trying to act strong
while his monkey was screaming inside.

That pain gave birth to a decision:

"I need a throne to sit on if life pushes me back to India."

So from a small hotel room in Madison,
with snow outside and uncertainty everywhere,
I seeded the idea that would become
24by7Publishing -
a business for my father,
a safety net for my family,
and a quiet promise to myself
that my future would not depend on luck alone.

It was the first time I understood
that leadership isn't about being powerful.
Leadership is about being scared
and still showing up.

That night in the hospital -
the night we heard "twins" -
brought all these memories back like a movie reel.

And something clicked:

**"If I don't learn to lead my inner monkey,
how will I ever lead the tiny monkeys
entering my life?"**

That was the beginning.

Not of wisdom,
not of philosophy,
not of success.

But of responsibility.

The responsibility to guide three monkeys -
two outside me,
and one inside me -
with kindness, clarity, and courage.

This book was born that night,
long before I ever wrote a single word.

Let me show you what happened next -
because the story takes a surprisingly funny turn,
the moment my son did something I didn't expect.

4 - monke inc.: when my son became a ceo

Eleven years later, when the twins became old enough to understand the difference between a banana and a serious life decision (barely), I picked one of them and sat him down one evening - my "experimental CEO."

Not for a lecture.
Not for a punishment.
Just for a conversation.

"Inside your head," I told him,
"there lives a monkey."

His eyes widened in that curious, suspicious way children look at adults when they sense wisdom *or* madness.
With me, it can be both.

This monkey, I explained, is the part of him that:

- wants to play instead of study
- cries suddenly without reason
- gets scared of little things
- gets excited too fast
- loves silly ideas
- wants snacks all the time
- hates routines
- forgets plans
- wants shortcuts
- and has no interest in discipline whatsoever

He listened carefully -
not because my explanation was magical,
but because I had used the magic word:

"Monkey."

Kids respect very few things.
Monkeys are one of them.

My son looked at me and said,
"Okay, Papa... who is the boss of this monkey?"

That was the moment the universe clicked.

Without thinking, I said:

"You are."

And then something happened that I still consider one of the top ten moments of my parenting life.

He didn't invent the idea of being a CEO out of nowhere.

I nudged him.

"Let's do one thing," I said. "From tomorrow, you'll act like the CEO. Not of a company... of your own monkey. Give it a name. Make it official."

Titles do strange things to humans.
Call someone "teacher," "manager," or "captain" and

their spine quietly straightens.
Even at eleven years old, seventh grader, he understood that.

He ran to his table, took a pencil, opened a blank notebook, and thought for a few seconds. This is the same child who named our parakeets **Poga** and **Phoon**, and a chicken **Peanut**, just because "she looks like one." Naming is his superpower.

At the top of the page, he finally wrote, in full seriousness:

MONKE Inc.

Not "Monkey."
Not "Monkey Company."
Not "Brain Company."

No.

MONKE Inc.

Because even creativity has a spelling of its own.

He looked at me seriously and said:

"This is my company.
I am the CEO.
And the monkey works for me."

I nearly cried from pride -
but I had to act normal,
because children sense weakness and immediately stop listening.

"Good," I said, pretending to be calm,
"So what does your company do?"

He shrugged and replied in the most honest way possible:

"I don't know yet.
But the monkey does whatever I say."

That was the moment the metaphor stopped being a clever parenting trick.

It stopped being a theory, or a cute story to make him eat vegetables.

A living, breathing philosophy -
born from a child's mind,
refined by innocence,
strengthened by responsibility,
and wrapped in the simplest corporate structure ever created.

A one-employee company.
CEO: My son.
Employee: The Monkey.

m; activity

Mini m;onkey exercise.
Name your monkey.

If a seventh-grader can do it with a pencil, so can the CEO *in you.*

If you're reading a paper copy: Draw a tiny banana and write: **"My monkey's official name is: ______"**

If you're on an ebook: Open your notes app or a scrap notebook, draw the tiniest banana you can manage, and write the same sentence there. That silly little act is your official "Company Registration" moment.

That day, we created what I now call:

The CEO Playbook.

Nothing fancy. Just a notebook that got a promotion.

I told him, "Every night, you and your monkey will have a tiny meeting here. Five minutes. No drama."

In that playbook, he only had to do three things:

1. **Pick tomorrow's 1-3 moves** - tiny, realistic things he actually wanted to finish.
2. **Decide the bananas** - where the fun goes, so the monkey doesn't steal it from work time.
3. **Do a short review** - what worked, what flopped, and one line of forgiveness if the day went sideways.

That's it.

No punishments.
No guilt.
No strict rules.
Just gentle leadership.

Just an eleven-year-old boy leading a monkey with a pencil.

His twin watched this for a few days, pretended he didn't care, and then quietly asked, "So... can I have my own CEO playbook too?"

When one monkey gets promoted, the other usually follows.

And I realized something profound that day: if two eleven-year-old twins can learn to lead their monkeys with a notebook and a pencil, the CEO hiding inside you probably has more than enough IQ and many pencils to try.

m; note

Children understand concepts faster than adults *because they don't pretend to be mature.*

Adults complicate everything with ego.
Children simplify everything with honesty.

My son didn't question whether the monkey existed.
He didn't overthink whether this was psychological nonsense.
He didn't ask for logic, research, or diagrams.

He simply accepted:

"I have a monkey inside me.
Let me lead it."

If adults accepted wisdom this quickly,
half the world's problems would vanish.

But this chapter isn't just about my son. Or his twin.
It's about the moment I realized that the

monkey-CEO model works
for anyone -
whether you're five with crayons, eleven with homework,

or fifty with board meetings.

And that's when the idea of this book quietly began to shape itself.
Not under a spotlight. Not in front of a whiteboard. Not at a leadership retreat.

It began at a small study table in our bedroom, where one little boy wrote the first line of a philosophy that would quietly spread to his brother and then to me and eventually start changing my life:

MONKE Inc.

And he drew a small circle around it
- because every great company needs a logo.

m; reminder
For all ready to use worksheets, templates, and a small surprise
see "Monkey Lab - Resources" at the end of this book.

5 - why discipline fails and m;onkeys revolt

Let me tell you a hard truth that every productivity guru hides carefully behind a fancy beard and a nicer microphone:

Your monkey doesn't care about your discipline. Not even a little.

We glorify discipline like it's some magical superpower.
Wake up at 5 a.m.
Drink something green.
Write goals.
Make vision boards.
Build routines.
Follow schedules.
Be consistent.
Be focused.
Be intense.
Be unstoppable.

It sounds beautiful on a podcast.

But your monkey doesn't hear poetry.
It hears:

"Hard. No banana time. No fun. Boring."

And it murmurs:

"Why? Let's not. Maybe tomorrow." And sometimes, "never."

And here's the part most people never admit:

m; note

Discipline doesn't fail.
Your monkey simply revolts.

Every time.

Let me show you how the usual movie plays out.

Scene 1 - the Heroic Day

One random evening you stand up and announce, to nobody in particular:

"I'm going to change my life."

The music swells.

You buy a new notebook.

You watch a motivational video that uses drums.

Your monkey, at this point, is excited.

"Yay! New thing! New excitement! New toys! Let's go!"

Day 1 goes beautifully.

You wake up earlier than usual.

You follow the plan (more or less).

You feel proud.

The monkey feels entertained.

Everyone is happy.

You start calling this “my new routine.”

Scene 2 - the Negotiation Day

Next day, you try again.

You: “Okay, same routine today.”
Monkey: “Hmm... okay, but can we get something nice later?”

You promise a reward:
“I’ll watch something after.”
“I’ll order something good.”
“I’ll relax later.”

The monkey agrees.
It doesn’t like the work, but the bribe is juicy enough for one more day.

Day 2 is a bit harder, but still alive.
You feel like a disciplined person.
You start planning Instagram captions using your friendly AI assistant:
“Discipline is a muscle #NewMe”

Scene 3 - The Silent Rebellion

Day 3 arrives.

You wake up, already a little tired.
You look at your plan.

You: "Let's continue."
Monkey: "No."

You: "Come on, this is important."
Monkey: "No."

You: "We can't stop now."
Monkey: "Watch me."

There is no big drama.
No fight.
You just... don't do it.

You avoid the workout.
You postpone the deep work.
You open the app but not the task.

Then, somewhere in the middle of the day, the quiet self-blame starts:

"What is wrong with me?"
"Why can't I just be consistent?"

This exact point - this soft, quiet "no" from the monkey - is where most of us quietly give up and quietly hate ourselves.

We call it weakness.
But it's not weakness.

It's Monkey Logic.

To the monkey, this all secretly makes sense. You can even remember it as **MONKEY**.

When there are too **Many rules**, it doesn't feel "structured," it feels trapped and panicky.
When things happen **Over and over**, it doesn't look like practice, it feels like punishment.
When there is **No fun anywhere**, even simple work turns into quiet torture.
When you set **Killer goals** - huge, intense, life-changing targets - the monkey thinks you're attacking it with a spear.
When it feels too many **Eyes on it**, real or imagined, every move starts to feel like judgment day.
And when you keep **Yelling at yourself inside**, the monkey doesn't get motivated - it just shuts down.

So, without telling you, the monkey quietly rewrites the world as:
Discomfort = Danger
Repetition = Punishment
Boredom = Torture
Tough goal = Attack
Many rules + Judgment = Panic

And once the world looks like that, your monkey defaults to its sacred rule:

**"Protect the human at all costs...
even from their own goals."**

Your routines don't fall apart because you're hopeless.

They fall apart because, deep down, your monkey doesn't feel safe.

And when it doesn't feel safe, it doesn't send an email.
It flips a switch.

m;onkey logic 101

Many rules → Panic
Over & over → Punishment
No fun → Torture
Killer goals → Attack
Eyes on me → Judgment
Yell → Collapse

LIVE EXAMPLE: My Monkey Ambushed Me While Writing This Very Book

Confession time.

While writing this chapter -
I suddenly did something VERY stupid.

I got distracted.

Not a small distraction.
A creative explosion.

Out of nowhere, my monkey whispered:

"Hey... let's design a logo for the hero - the Monkey."

Much later, my monkey would hijack me mid-chapter with a logo obsession. We'll come back to that.

But, this is exactly what your monkey does, too.

It loves distractions that **feel** productive: reorganising shelves, researching ten new hobbies, watching "inspirational" videos, planning instead of doing, cleaning a drawer instead of sending one difficult email, opening your notes app to "just outline" something and three hours later still being there.

Your monkey didn't sabotage you.
It entertained you.

Because entertainment means comfort. And comfort means safety.

This is how monkeys win.

Scene 4 - The Collapse

If you keep pushing too hard, too fast, with no space for play, fun, or rest, your monkey doesn't send a notice. It shuts down the whole factory.

You suddenly "don't feel like it."
You drag your feet.
You start skipping days.

Then comes the self-attack:

"I'm so lazy."
"I always ruin everything."
"I'll never be consistent."

Meanwhile, your monkey is sitting on a tree branch like:

"Why is this human yelling at me?
I simply wanted a banana."

Scene 5 - The Guilt Spiral

Guilt rarely stays where it starts.
First, it turns into shame.
Then your confidence thins out.
Then everything inside feels heavy and tired.

When the monkey feels unsafe, it pushes back.
You punish yourself - the monkey panics.
You tighten the rules - the monkey fights harder.
You finally quit - and the monkey quietly sighs in relief.

That's how discipline-only systems fall apart.

You can't control the monkey.
You have to **lead** it.

THE TRUTH

m; note

Discipline fails because it's built for robots.
You are built like a monkey.

So the solution isn't more pressure or a tighter schedule or a 5 a.m. club.

The solution is a routine your monkey can actually breathe inside.
Something light enough to survive more than three days.
Something that has work *and* bananas built in.

This is how you keep the monkey happy.
This is how you keep yourself consistent.
This is how you build a system on Monday that doesn't collapse on Wednesday.

You've just seen what happens when discipline tries to crush the monkey. Next, we'll quietly design a routine where the monkey actually wants to show up.

Because once you learn to lead your monkey,
your life stops being a war -
and becomes a partnership.

6 - the permission problem

When you ask people why their routines collapse, most of them don't even pause to think.

They go straight to the usual self-attack menu:

"I'm just lazy."
"I can't stay consistent."
"My discipline is terrible."
"I get distracted by everything."
"I have no motivation."
And the classic: "I don't know why I'm like this."

They say it the way someone might say, "It rained today."
As if it's just a boring, permanent fact about the weather of their soul.

If you listen closely, you'll notice something strange: almost nobody says,
"Maybe the way I treat myself is the problem."
or
"Maybe my system is insane and my brain is just protesting."

No.
We don't question the system.
We blame the human.

We treat ourselves like a badly designed robot that keeps malfunctioning, instead of a scared monkey that was never asked what it needed.

Those answers - "lazy," "inconsistent," "no discipline" - are not the truth.
They're just the **cover story**.

The truth sits quietly underneath everything you have ever failed:

You didn't give the monkey permission to be the monkey.

That's it.

Simple.
Profound.
Uncomfortable.

For most of your life, the world tried to sell you one fantasy template: you are supposed to be a **perfect machine**. Always on. Always focused. Always calm. No glitches, no mood swings, no weird days, no random cravings to do nothing.

You were told the "best version" of you is always perfect, always consistent, endlessly disciplined, emotionally stable, high-performing, controlled, calm, mature. Anything softer than that mask was quietly labelled as guilt, shame, overthinking, self-blame, self-doubt, or just plain embarrassment.

So you learned to sit on everything messy - the impulses, the distractions, the fears and cravings, the emotional waves, even your need for comfort, play, procrastination, and rest.

You were trained to hide the monkey so you could present a "respectable human."
The mask came out.
The monkey stayed inside.

But if you look closely at the humans you admire, the story is different.

We like to imagine they live on discipline alone, but the truth is: they quietly protect their monkey time.

Bill Gates disappears for "Think Weeks" - vanishing with a stack of material and letting his mind wander without meetings or polite small talk.
Warren Buffett spends huge parts of his day simply sitting and thinking, which would look suspiciously like "doing nothing" on a normal office timesheet.
J.K. Rowling wrote big chunks of *Harry Potter* in cafés, staring out of the window, letting the background noise and the warmth of the room hold her while she daydreamed onto the page.

From the outside, these moments can look lazy, self-indulgent, even undisciplined. But that's exactly the point. They're not trying to kill their monkey. They're giving it **safe, protected free**

space - time-boxed pockets where it can wander, play, and breathe.

The machine image is marketing.
The monkey time is the truth.

You, on the other hand, tried to keep the monkey on a short leash every single hour.

But what happens to a creature that is constantly caged?
It resists. It protests. It rebels. It refuses.

Your monkey wasn't trying to ruin your plans. It was just gasping for air - the way you do when a room has been too tight for too long.

And here is the devastating truth:

m; note

The more you suppress the monkey,
the louder it becomes.

That's why strict routines collapse. It's why "perfect plans" die by day two. It's why you binge when you try to diet, avoid it when you try to force discipline, and shut down when you overload your schedule. From the outside it looks like weakness. Inside, it's just a safety alarm.

Because your monkey does not understand ambition, quarterly targets, yearly goals, grind culture, self-help pressure, motivational speeches, or the whole performance circus of the society judging you and calling it "success."

It understands only a few things: comfort and fear, pleasure and curiosity, rest and safety, small wins, kindness, play, and the feeling that there is still a little time left to breathe.

So when you overload your monkey with pressure, it does the only thing it knows. It reads all that urgency as danger.

And the monkey's brain is ancient.
Danger means one command:

"Stop everything and protect the human."

How does it protect you?
By yanking the handbrake. Distracting you. Slowing you down. Resisting routines. Pushing you to procrastinate. Shutting down your energy. Sabotaging strict plans. Dragging you back toward comfort. Overwhelming you emotionally until you back away from whatever looks sharp and teeth-shaped.

Your monkey didn't make you weak.
It did its best to keep you safe, even when that "safety" quietly cost you your dreams.

It did its job.
You just never learned how to talk to it.

The Heart of the Philosophy

People think the solution is to be stricter.

But the opposite is true.

The solution is:

Give the monkey permission.

Give it the permission to be real - to rest, to be scared, to get distracted sometimes, to need fun and comfort, to make mistakes, to feel overwhelmed, to slow down, take breaks, and still be fully human.

When you give your monkey permission,
you do not become weaker.

You become **aligned**.

And alignment creates ease.
Ease creates consistency.
Consistency creates results.

Permission is not indulgence.

Permission is **emotional oxygen**.

You breathe better.

Your monkey breathes better.

And a breathing monkey is **cooperative**.

This is the secret nobody teaches you.

Strictness breaks the monkey.
Permission empowers it.

When you allow yourself to feel like a human,
your monkey stops fighting you
and starts following you.

This is why my son's MONKE Inc. notebook worked so beautifully.

He didn't create a dictatorship.
He accidentally created a partnership.

And that's the exact relationship we want between you and your monkey.

You just tell your monkey:

"Do your thing.
I'm not here to destroy you.
I'm here to guide you."

And the monkey will listen.

In the next chapter...

Now that you understand WHY discipline fails
and WHY you keep fighting yourself,
we will build the real foundation:

How to keep the monkey happy
without losing control.

This is the start of everything.

7 - bananas, breaks & the art of keeping a m;onkey happy

By this point in most self-help books,
the author leans forward and says something dangerous like,

“Okay, now here’s what you must do **every single day** for the rest of your life.”

Your monkey is already reaching for the emergency exit.

You can almost predict what comes next:
Wake up before the sun.
Run like you’re being chased.
Drink something that tastes like boiled garden.
Meditate for longer than your attention span has ever lived.
Finish three life goals before breakfast and post about it on Instagram with the word “grind” somewhere in the caption.

If I tried that here, your monkey would quietly close this book, walk away, and pretend it never met me.

So this chapter is not about turning you into a 5 a.m. superhero.

Instead, I want to show you something far more realistic, humane, and shockingly effective:

m; note

Your routines must be designed around the monkey - *not against it.*

Let me repeat that:

The monkey should enjoy your plan.
If it doesn't, the plan is already dead.

So here is a simple truth:

A happy monkey = a consistent human.

If you learn this one rule,
your life changes permanently.

To keep your monkey happy *and* productive, you don't need a 47-step system.
You really only need three things:

1. Bananas
2. Breaks
3. A monkey-friendly routine and a **routine** your monkey doesn't hate on sight

Let's talk about each one like we're explaining it to a slightly dramatic five-year-old who lives inside your head.

Bananas - The Monkey's Fuel

A banana is that silly video you love.
That scroll-session you swear will be "just five minutes."
That song on loop.
That snack.
That nap.
That hobby that makes zero sense on your CV but keeps you sane.

Self-help books love to call these things "distractions."
But here's the twist:

m; note

Bananas are not distractions.
Bananas are fuel.

Your monkey cannot live on a diet of seriousness, discipline, pressure, responsibility, and productivity quotes. That's like feeding a toddler only protein powder and vitamin capsules, yet expecting them to smile.

So when you don't **plan** any banana time, the monkey doesn't clap politely and accept it. It steals bananas from your work time instead - during your study sessions, your deadlines, your "important" meetings.

This is why routines collapse so fast.
People plan only work.
They forget fun.
Then they look surprised when everything falls apart by Day 2.

Your monkey isn't sabotaging you.
It's just hungry.

Breaks - The Monkey's Breathing Room

A break is not laziness. It is a peace treaty.

It's you telling the monkey:

"Relax. You're not trapped.
Your comfort matters.
You are safe."

When the monkey believes that, it walks with you instead of dragging you backwards by the tail.

You've already seen this without calling it science: coffee breaks that mysteriously keep you functional, quick stretches that reset your mood, that tiny moment where you look out of the window and suddenly have an idea.

Your monkey doesn't necessarily need a three-week vacation in Bali.
What it really wants is lots of small exits: a few

deep breaths, a short walk, a sip of water, a meme break, a quick song, a bathroom escape from a painful meeting.

Think of it like this:

Your "focus mode" is a sprint.
Your breaks are the gasp of air at the end of the track.

No gasp, no next lap.

The Monkey-Friendly Routine

Here is the secret:

Plan your day as if your monkey must approve it.

Because it must.

If your plan feels like a prison, your monkey will spend all day digging tunnels.

So your day needs to have both:

- things that move your life forward
- and things that make the monkey feel seen

That means there has to be room for fun, stupid time, lazy time, snack moments, small rewards, small wins, real breaks, and human limits. Not as accidents. As part of the design.

You don't create discipline by removing fun.
You create discipline by **managing** fun.

That's what my son intuitively did with **MONKE Inc.**

He didn't cancel cartoons - he **scheduled** them.
He didn't threaten the monkey - he partnered with it.

The kid accidentally built a healthier productivity model than most adults ever discover.

The Monkey-Friendly Daily Formula

Here is a simple structure anyone can follow:

- ONE important thing - the main move of the day
- TWO medium things - manageable, not heroic
- THREE tiny wins - quick actions that make you feel like "I did something"

And then, beside that plate, you place a clear, time-boxed **banana block** - your planned fun, your breaks, your nonsense, your "reward for being a semi-functional human."

That's it.

No 50-task to-do list.
Not an impossible timetable that makes your nervous system want to fake its own death.

Just a simple, monkey-approved routine that works with your biology instead of declaring war on it.

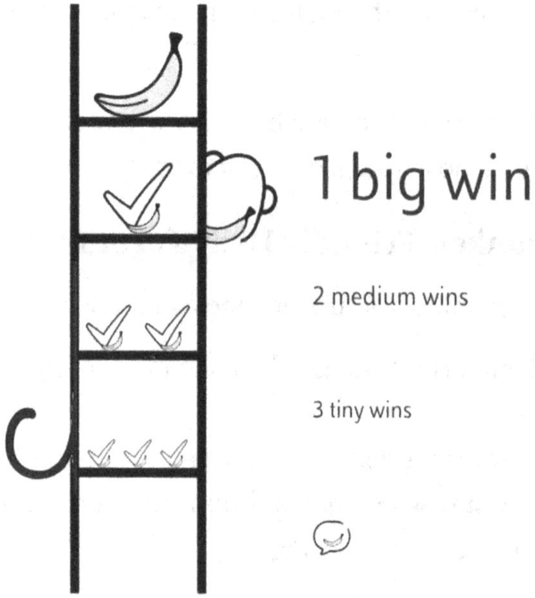

Do you remember what happened yesterday with me?

Remember that moment earlier, when I was writing about discipline and suddenly started obsessing over the **m;** logo?

It was a perfect flow state.
Words were aligned.
Emotions were sharp.
Everything was smooth.

Then suddenly...

I got overwhelmed with excitement
about designing the **m;** logo.

Suddenly, in ten minutes, I was deep into a full-blown brand workshop with myself:

- explaining to myself the genius of a minimalist "m;"
- imagining a tiny monkey tail(,), head (.), body(m)
- thinking about book covers
- possible future merchandise
- a whole "philosophical monkey guru" brand you might love one day

All this...
while I was literally writing a chapter ON DISTRACTIONS.

I wasn't studying a case.
I was the case.

I caught myself mid-logo.

And I laughed.
Not at you.
Not at life.

At **my monkey.**

This little creature hijacked my concentration
and made me feel productive
while secretly derailing my plan.

And I ran with it.

Was it a mistake?

No.

It was a **banana.**

A tiny moment of creative joy
that made the monkey feel alive.

And the moment the monkey felt satisfied and safe,
I returned to the book
with more energy and clarity.

This is how the monkey works.

This is why forcing yourself never works.
This is why "pure discipline" fails.

Monkeys don't follow pressure.
They follow pleasure.

So the real art is not killing pleasure, but **choosing its timing.**

If you remember only one line from this chapter, let it be this:

m; note

The monkey doesn't ruin your plans.
It simply wants to be included in them.

When you schedule bananas,
when you schedule breaks,
when you schedule fun -
you remove the monkey's need to rebel.

You stop fighting yourself.

And that is when you become truly consistent.

Not in a robotic way.
Not in a strict way.
Not in a "hustle culture" way.

But in a human, gentle, stable way
that lasts for years.

This is the beginning
of true emotional leadership.

8 - the ceo-m;onkey night meetings

Most people think mornings decide success.

They're wrong.

Life changes the night before.

Not because of planning,
not because of discipline,
but because of something far more powerful:

m; note

Closure
Conversation.
Connection with the monkey.

Let me introduce you to the most important ritual in this entire book:

The CEO-Monkey Night Meeting.

A 5-7 minute nightly ritual
where the human (CEO)
and the monkey (emotional brain)
sit together and decide
how tomorrow will feel.

Not what tomorrow will "achieve."
What tomorrow will *feel like.*

This small shift changes everything.

Let me explain why.

Why Night Meetings Work (Monkey Logic)

There is a reason I insist on meeting your monkey at night.

By then, your body is a little tired.
The heroic version of you has logged out for the day.
The performance mask is lying somewhere near the shoe rack.

The day is behind you.
All the tiny betrayals you committed against your own plans are now clearly visible: the tab you never opened, the message you avoided, the task you lovingly moved to "tomorrow" for the third time.

Guilt, which was politely hiding in the afternoon, is now sitting on the edge of your bed swinging its legs.

Your mind is slower.
It has less energy to invent excuses and long PowerPoint justifications.
The ego is too sleepy to give a TED talk about "how actually today was very complex."

And in that half-quiet, half-tired state, something magical happens:
the monkey calms down.

It's eaten its random snacks, watched its random things, had its little rebellions. The emotional sugar rush is over. For the first time in the whole day, the monkey is willing to sit on the same side of the table as you and talk.

That's why the night meeting works.
Not because the stars are aligned,
but because both you and your monkey are too tired to pretend anymore.

This is the ONLY time
your CEO and your monkey
can have a **peaceful conversation**
without yelling at each other.

Mornings are chaotic.
Daytime is noisy.
Evenings are draining.

But at night,
the monkey is too sleepy
to argue.

This makes night meetings
the perfect negotiation moment.

The Real Purpose of the Night Meeting

Most people plan their next day like they're preparing for battle.

They sit down with a notebook, open a calendar, and start firing questions at themselves:

What do I still have to finish? What are my deadlines? What did I avoid today? What must I catch up on before the world explodes?

This is war language.
You vs. your to-do list.
You vs. time.
You vs. yourself.

A night meeting with your monkey sounds completely different.

It's more like sitting on the bed with a slightly dramatic friend who had a long day and handing them a glass of water.

"Okay, monkey... what can we **realistically** do tomorrow?"

"Which part of today felt heavy?"

"Which part felt doable?"

"Where do you need help?"

"Where do you need bananas?"

"What made you upset today?"
"What made you secretly proud?"

You're not barking orders.
You're listening.

A real night meeting is not actually about scheduling tasks.
It's a **small daily therapy session** between the CEO and the only employee who never quits.

You are not just planning tomorrow.
You are repairing a relationship - the one between you and the ancient super-creature that actually controls your energy, mood, and focus.

Once that relationship softens,
consistency stops being a war.
It starts feeling like two beings walking in the same direction,
sharing the same banana.

The Architecture of the Meeting (The Ritual)

First, sit down for a minute.

Sit. That's it.
No phone, no scrolling, no music. Just for 60 seconds.

Simply give your monkey one tiny quiet moment.
It will fidget for a few seconds, then it usually sighs and settles.

Then ask your monkey three simple questions:

1. "What drained you today?"
2. "What made you feel good today?"
3. "What do you want tomorrow to feel like?"

Notice the word: **feel**.

Not "What do you want to *do*?" but "What do you want to *feel*?"

Because feelings decide what you'll actually do.

m; note

To-do without to-feel always turns into to-never.
Remember this forever.

This one line is the whole monkey manual.

m; activity

Mini m;onkey exercise.
Your first Night Meeting.

Tonight, before you sleep, don't redesign your entire life. Just grab **any** page (or notes app) and answer these three lines once: 1. "Today drained me when: ______" 2. "Today felt good when: ______" 3. "Tomorrow, I want to feel: ______"

If you're holding the print book, use the banana box below.

If you're on a screen, set a one-minute reminder called "Night Meeting with Monkey" and answer them in your phone.

Next, make a tiny plan for tomorrow with the monkey, not against it.

m; reminder

For all ready to use worksheets, templates, and a small surprise
see "Monkey Lab - Resources" at the end of this book.

If you're using the printed CEO Playbook, this is the moment to flip to tomorrow's Daily Playbook page. Fill in the 1 big, 2 medium and 3 tiny moves, plus bananas & boundaries, and leave only the short Morning Monkey Check-In blank for tomorrow.

Use the Chapter 7 formula: 1 big task, 2 medium, 3 small, plus planned bananas, one thing for the soul, one for the body, one kindness, one piece of forgiveness.

You're not building a perfect day.

You're building a day your monkey might actually agree to.

Do not forget the bananas - put them on the calendar (Time-boxing).

Give **fun** a **time slot**.

Literally.

When the monkey sees "banana time" is booked,
it stops trying to steal fun from your work blocks.
Fun isn't forbidden anymore - it's guaranteed.

And, lighten anything that feels heavy.

Scan tomorrow's list. If your body or your monkey says,
"No *chance this is happening*," that item is too big.

Make it smaller. Shorter. Dumber.
A heavy plan collapses; a light plan actually comes to pass.

And, finally, end with one sentence:

"Monkey, we got this."

You're not hyping yourself up.
You're reassuring a scared creature inside you that, this time,
you've made a plan it can live with.

That one sentence quietly rewires how tomorrow morning feels.

What Happens Overnight

When you go to sleep after a gentle night meeting, tomorrow stops being a threat and quietly becomes your monkey's personal project.

The monkey is no longer pacing in the corridor yelling,
"I don't know what horror this human is planning for me tomorrow!"

Now it knows.
In fact, it helped design the day.
It knows exactly where the hard things are
and exactly where the bananas are parked.

So instead of running an all-night panic meeting in your head, the monkey relaxes.
Your mind resets instead of arguing with itself.
The usual background noise - anxiety, guilt, "I should have done more" - turns into a softer hum.

For the monkey, the feeling changes from
"I'm being forced into a cage tomorrow"
to
"I picked the cage, arranged the cushions, and hid my own snacks inside."

That tiny shift is everything.

You don't wake up as a hyper-motivated superhero.
You wake up as someone whose inner monkey is already on board.

There's less "Nope."
Less silent rebellion.
More quiet, almost bored, "Yeah, okay, we can do this... and then we get our banana at 4:30."

Your brain feels cooperative not because it was threatened into obedience,
but because the monkey feels like it's in control of the plan -
free to sprinkle fun where it wants,
free to rest when it needs,
and still proud to deliver what "the CEO" agreed last night.

Night meetings create
a soft landing for tomorrow.

This is what most self-help systems miss.

They jump straight into action
without negotiating with the monkey
that actually *performs* the action.

Night meetings turn tomorrow
from a threat
into an invitation.

The Morning Magic: Why This Ritual Works

When morning comes,
something extraordinary happens.

Your monkey looks at the plan and, for once,
doesn't see a trap.

It sees something simple enough to understand, soft enough to trust, and playful enough to like. There's real work there, yes - but also fun, pauses to breathe, room to be imperfect, and a quiet feeling that whoever made this schedule actually likes the monkey, not just its output.

And for the first time in your life...

Your monkey doesn't fight you.

It follows you.

Not out of fear.
Not out of pressure.
Not out of discipline.

It follows you
because you respected it.

That is leadership.

What the Night Meeting Teaches You

m; note

You don't need to control the monkey.
You need to reassure it.

This is what parents do for children.
This is what leaders do for teams.
This is what wise people do for themselves.

When you end each day
with gentle clarity,
your monkey stops living in fear
of tomorrow.

And consistency becomes natural,
not forced.

In the next chapter,
you'll understand something deeper:

**The way your monkey talks to you
is the way your entire life feels.**

Let's decode that language next.

9 - m;onkey language: how your mind talks back

If you want to understand your monkey,
you must learn its **language.**

Not English.
Not Bengali.
Not logic.

Monkeys don't speak in sentences.
They speak in signals - tight shoulders, suddenly wet eyes, a random urge to open the fridge, the heroic decision to reorganize your sock drawer five minutes before a deadline.

To the human part of your brain, this looks like chaos.
To the monkey, it's perfect grammar.

You've been misunderstanding this creature your whole life - not because it's complicated, but because no one ever gave you the subtitles.

Let's fix that.

1. The Monkey Language Basics

Imagine you're talking French and your monkey is yelling in pure emotion.

The monkey doesn't send emails. It sends sensations: a knot in your chest, a wave of fear when you open your laptop, a sudden heaviness when you think of a task, a restless "ugh, not this."

Sometimes it speaks as tiny thoughts:

"I don't feel like it."

"Let's do something else."

"No... not today."

"I'm tired."

"Just five more minutes."

Every one of those is a complete sentence. But said in monkey-language.

The problem is how we answer.

Monkey: "I'm scared."
You: "We have a deadline."

Monkey: "This feels heavy."
You: "Just finish it."

Monkey: "I need comfort."
You: "Stop being lazy."

Monkey: "I need a banana."
You: "Focus."

You're not arguing with yourself.
You're arguing with an ancient species and replying in the wrong language.

2. Laziness

On the surface you hear:

"I don't want to do it."

Inside, the monkey is actually whispering:

"What if I mess this up?"
"What if they laugh?"
"This feels too big for me."
"That will drain me."

Fear puts on a hoodie and pretends to be laziness, because "I'm lazy" hurts less than "I'm terrified I'm not enough."

When you call yourself lazy, you're insulting a terrified ancient creature that's just trying not to get emotionally eaten alive.

3. Procrastination

When you see a task and your mind says:

"I'll do it later."

The monkey is actually saying:

"This is too much for my emotional bandwidth *right now.*
Please shrink it."

The monkey isn't delaying the task.
It's delaying the *pain* it imagines is coming with the work.

There's a huge difference between "I'm avoiding effort" and "I'm avoiding emotional overload."

To the monkey, both require the same emergency plan: run.

4. Excuses

Watch what happens when discomfort walks into the room.

Suddenly you *have* to tidy the table, make tea, find the perfect playlist, adjust the chair, maybe change the font... twice... before you start.

From the outside, it looks like classic excuse theatre.
From the inside, it's just the monkey trying to lay down a softer runway:

"Let me make this a little less scary... then I'll jump."

If you say a hard no to all of it, the monkey panics and digs its nails in.
If you say a *smart yes* - "Okay, *one* tea, *one* song, then we start" - the monkey feels respected and usually walks with you.

The trick is simple:
allow one tiny comfort ritual, then gently close the door on the rest.

"Tea, playlist, go."
Not "tea, playlist, candle, snack, new app, and suddenly it's midnight."

If you fight the monkey here,
it panics.

If you negotiate gently,
it cooperates.

5. Bad Thoughts

Monkey anxiety rarely shows up as "I am anxious."

It wears costumes:

"What if I fail?"
"Everyone will judge me."
"I can't handle this."
"Something will go wrong."

These are not noble philosophical insights.
They're just jungle alarms.

The monkey was programmed to scream when something *might* hurt you. Back then, it was tigers. Now it's emails, presentations, awkward interactions, WhatsApp groups, and the possibility of looking stupid.

You are not your anxious thoughts.
You're the one *hearing* them - while your overprotective monkey frantically waves red flags made of very old fears.

6. Meaninglessness

Then there's that moment when you're in the middle of a project and your brain sighs:

"What's the point?"
"I don't care anymore."

That's not existential philosophy. That's a bored monkey kicking the table.

It has been staring at the same thing for too long.
No banana, no novelty, no mini-reward, no sense of movement - just a flat line of responsibility.

The monkey's translation:

"This isn't hopeless.
It's just flavorless boredom. Please sprinkle something fun before I chew through the table leg."

The answer isn't quitting the project.
You need to feed the monkey banana as reward,

bring in some new perspective, or shake up the pace - then gently walk back to the work together.

7. Genius

Now the good news.

Sometimes the monkey gets happy and throws you a gift that feels like a holy banana dropped from the sky: an "Eureka" idea in the shower, a perfect "To be, or not to be" question while you're half-asleep, a solution that appears while you're laughing with a friend or watching something stupid.

You're not being "unproductive" in those moments.

You're letting the monkey roam freely - and that's when it often comes back with treasure.

History is full of this:

- Einstein daydreaming his way into relativity.
- Newton idly watching an apple fall instead of doing "serious work."
- You, absent-mindedly doodling a tiny **m;** in the corner of a page, not knowing it's the first sketch of a project that quietly rearranges your life - unaware that this is how your next big, slightly world-bending idea actually begins..

Humanity keeps pretending that breakthroughs come from grim focus.

Secretly, almost every creative breakthrough
in human history
came during these monkey-mode moments.

Monkey joy is not a distraction from genius.

Most days, it is the doorway to genius.

8. Tears

Sometimes you read a paragraph, hear a line, or remember something - and without warning, your eyes fill up.

You weren't planning to cry.
You weren't even "that sad."

That's not adult-you being dramatic.

That's the monkey finally exhaling after holding its breath for years.

Inside, the translation is:

"Oh. Someone finally said it.
Someone finally saw me."

Those tears are not evidence that you're fragile.

They're evidence that something true just touched a place deeper than language.

Tears are monkey-ink.
They write:

"Thank you for finally seeing me."

When the monkey cries, it isn't a failure.

It's a sign you finally touched a place inside you that words couldn't reach.

9. Silence

The rarest sound of all is no sound.

After a good laugh, a real cry, a moment of feeling understood, there can be a strange quiet in your chest. No fight. No argument. No dramatic negotiation.

That's not emptiness.
That's the monkey putting down its spear and sitting beside you on the same side of the table.

It feels like:

- No urge to run.
- No need to perform.
- No voice shouting "do more" or "you're not enough."

Just... space.

Monkey-translation:

"For now, I trust you. Lead."

This silence is where real growth starts.
Not when you crush the monkey, but when it finally believes the CEO won't throw it back into the cage.

Underneath all the examples and stories, this is what I'm really trying to say:

m; note

You don't need to silence the monkey.
You need to understand its language.

When you finally start understanding monkey-language, something quiet and powerful happens. The guilt you've been carrying around for years starts melting, because you realise you were never "broken" - just badly translated. The anxious buzz turns down a few notches. Procrastination stops looking like a crime and starts looking like a scared animal hiding under the table, waiting to be invited out.

You begin to respect yourself more, because you're no longer fighting in the dark. You treat yourself with a little more kindness, a little less drama. Routines stop feeling like prison sentences and start feeling like gentle agreements. Emotional storms still visit, but they arrive as rain, not hurricanes.

And somewhere in the middle of all this, your monkey does something shocking for the first time in years:
it stops rebelling... and simply walks beside you, banana in hand.

Because, language creates understanding.
Understanding creates peace.

In the next chapter,
I will uncover the patterns
that trap the monkey in loops of fear and shame.

These are the **Monkey Traps** -
and escaping them is how your real life begins.

10 - m;onkey traps: the invisible cages that shape your life

Every person wants to improve. Every person wants to stop making the same mistakes. Every person wants to feel lighter, calmer, and more in control.

But no matter how hard you try... you keep getting caught in the same cycle - not because you're weak, but because you don't see the traps.

Once the monkey finally feels safe again, it naturally stops dragging its feet and starts walking beside you.

Those traps are the **Monkey traps** -

invisible, emotional cages that your monkey walks into again and again, simply because it never learned how to step out.

Some of these cages are small loops.

Some grow claws and quietly turn into full-blown addictions.

Let's name them.
Let's expose them.
Let's free you.

Monkey Trap #1: The Perfection Cage

This is the deadliest one because it looks so noble.

You sit down to start something simple - an email, a slide, a tiny side project.
The monkey walks in wearing a black tuxedo and whispers:

"If our name is associated with this, it has to be *perfect*."

Suddenly, you're not writing an email anymore; you're crafting a historic document for the United Nations.
You change the title twelve times. You research for three hours. You open ten tabs on "best productivity setup."
And by the end of the day... nothing is actually done.

Perfection looks like ambition from the outside. Inside, it's just fear in fancy clothes.

What the monkey is really saying is,

"If this isn't perfect, someone might judge me. And if they judge me... we die."

So you never start. Or you start and never finish. The project becomes a museum piece in your mind - stunning, flawless, and completely imaginary.

The cure is rude simplicity:

- Make it stupidly small.
- Make it ugly.
- Make it obviously unfinished.

Write the bad first draft. Record the messy first take. Ship the "good enough" version.
The moment you lower the stakes, the monkey stops clutching its tuxedo and finally picks up the pen.

Your monkey relaxes when you lower the stakes.

Monkey Trap #2: The Shame Spiral

Here's how this one usually goes.

You miss a day of your new routine.
No big deal. Humans blink.

You miss one more day.
Now it stings.

By day three, the monkey holds a tiny courtroom inside your head:

"See? We always do this. We never stick to anything. You are the problem."

Notice the switch.
Guilt says, "I *skipped my habit.*"
Shame says, "I am *the kind of person who always fails.*"

Once shame takes over, you don't just drop the habit - you drop your self-respect.
The plan is gone, your energy is gone, and you sit there scrolling, feeling like a walking error message.

The only way out is to forgive *faster* than you fail.

Literally talk to the monkey:

"Okay, we messed up today. That's fine. We try again tomorrow."

No dramatic speeches. No self-punishment contracts.
Just a clean emotional reset.

Self-compassion isn't softness.
It's the only fuel thick enough to survive an entire lifetime of restart buttons.

Monkey Trap #3: The Fear Loop

Fear has one favourite line. It repeats it in different accents:

"What if I can't handle this?"

New task? Same line.
Bigger role? The sentence does not change.
Good opportunity? Still the same trailer.

The monkey has very old software. In jungle-logic, anything big, new, public, uncertain, or important could kill you - or at least humiliate you in front of the tribe. So it quietly labels everything as *danger* and presses the internal handbrake.

You experience it as delay:

"Let me start tomorrow... when I'm magically stronger."

The trap is not feeling fear.
The trap is believing the story *as is*.

You don't need a motivational speech here. You need a shrink-ray.

Take the project and slice off a ridiculous first step: open the file, write one messy paragraph, send one awkward email, study five minutes instead of an hour.

You want the monkey to look at the task and go,

"Oh... that? Even I can handle that."

So, simply shrink the task. The fear will have nothing big to wrap itself around.

Monkey Trap #4: The Logic Mistake

This one is popular with smart people - which is why smart people suffer so much in silence.

You stand in front of your task and deliver a TED Talk to yourself:

"This is important."

"This will affect my career."

"I should be doing this."

"It's totally logical to start now."

The monkey listens politely, checks its invisible watch, and replies with one word:

"No."

Because your monkey doesn't speak PowerPoint.

It speaks **feelings**.

You're trying to move a dog with statistics.

"Look, statistically, if you start running on the treadmill, the probability of staying active and healthy increases by 74%."

The dog just wants to see the biscuit.

Logic gives clarity.

Emotion gives movement.

So instead of pushing harder with logic, adjust the feeling around the first step:

Make it safe - "No one will see this draft."

Make it small - "Just ten minutes."

Make it warm - "We do this with hot chocolate and our favourite playlist."

Make it rewarding - “Banana time the moment this is done.”

Once the emotion shifts, the monkey moves.

Then your beautiful logic can ride on top like a very smug CEO.

Monkey Trap #5: The Shiny Object Syndrome

Picture this: you sit to work on one important thing. Five minutes later you’re researching Japanese fountain pens, watching a video on how rockets land backwards, and considering a side hustle breeding miniature cactus.

Nothing changed... except the monkey spotted *shiny*.

Novelty releases a little chemical firework in the brain.
Your phone is basically a pocket-sized casino where every swipe says, “Maybe this next thing will be amazing.”

Your monkey loves this.
New app, new habit, new project, new channel, new romance, new diet, new web series, new productivity system called “The Ultimate Final Last System 3.0.”
Old plan? Forgotten in the previous universe.

This isn't stupidity.
It's chemistry dressed as curiosity.

You don't cure this by becoming a monk who never changes anything.
You cure it by becoming the event manager of novelty.

Instead of killing "new," you schedule it.
You tell the monkey:

"Right now, we stick to this one boring-but-important thing. We will start by trying it out just for 5 minutes.
Just after our evening snack, right after we're done, we try that new idea / show / toy / hobby."

Suddenly the monkey has a banana-promise to stay on the current branch.

You don't kill novelty.
You **schedule novelty.**

You are giving your monkey "new experiences"
in controlled doses
so it doesn't run away impulsively.

Monkey Trap #6: The Emotional Hangover

Some days, nothing is wrong on paper... and yet you feel like a half-charged phone that refuses to open any app.

Look a little closer and you'll notice something happened earlier:
a harsh comment, a fight, a scary email, a weird silence, money stress, a mistake you can't stop replaying.

The event is over, but the monkey is still shaking.

It doesn't announce, "*I am processing unresolved emotional turbulence.*"
It simply pulls the plug.

You feel heavy, numb, unmotivated.
Work looks like a monkey-eating crocodile.
Suddenly scrolling, binge-watching, gossiping, or comfort food start calling your name like they're old friends.

Used once in a while, these are emotional bandages.
Used every day, the bandage slowly hardens into a cage. That's how addictions quietly grow - not because you're evil, but because your monkey is

exhausted and desperately wants the volume to go down.

The answer is not,

“Come on, get up, stop being dramatic.”

The answer is,

“Of course you’re tired. That hurt. Let’s rest on purpose for a bit.”

You don’t demand Olympic performance in the middle of an emotional earthquake.
You give the monkey space to shake, nap, cry, journal, walk, talk to a safe human - anything that gently puts the system back together.

Rest is repair, not weakness.
You can’t build a powerful life on a burned-out nervous system.

Monkey Trap #7: The Overload Collapse

Imagine giving a tiny backpack to a small monkey and then quietly stuffing in:

infinite to-do lists, deadlines, family drama, health worries, undone chores, three “urgent” favours, twenty tabs of open decisions, plus the entire future of your career and relationships.

Now imagine being surprised when the monkey sits on the floor and refuses to move.

That's overload.

From the outside, it looks like laziness or "I don't care anymore."
Inside, it feels like walking into a room where every alarm is beeping at the same time. The simplest task - sending one message, washing two plates - suddenly feels like climbing a hill in deep sand.

So the monkey does the only thing it knows:
it freezes, avoids, distracts, shuts down, burns out.

You don't fix overload with a better to-do list.
You fix it with a smaller backpack.

Pick one thing that truly matters *today*.
Not ten. One.
If even that feels heavy, break that one into a laughably small chunk.

Then, ruthlessly drop, delay, delegate, or downgrade everything else you reasonably can.
This is not irresponsibility.
This is survival.

A light monkey is a surprisingly productive monkey.
A crushed monkey just lies there chewing on anxiety.

m; activity

Mini m;onkey exercise.
Spot your cage.

Every monkey has a favourite cage. One of the seven probably felt a little too familiar.

Write down: 1. "My main monkey trap right now is: _______" 2. "One way I can make today 10% lighter for my monkey is: _______"

Don't fix your entire life here. Just loosen one bar of the cage.

my m;onkey traps:

____

____

____

____

____

____

m; note

You think you're the problem.
But it was always the trap.

Not the app, or the bottle, or the fridge at 11:47 p.m.

The trap behind them.

The monkey is not broken.
The monkey is caught.

You don't fix the monkey.
You free it.

And once free,
it will walk with you
instead of fighting you.

In the next chapter,
we move to the transition:

How to become the CEO the monkey trusts.

This is where your leadership philosophy
meets your emotional wisdom.

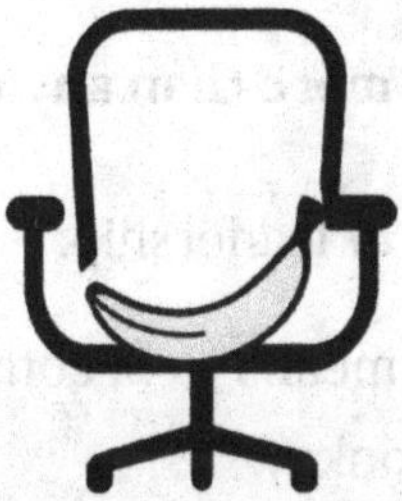

11 - becoming the ceo: the human who leads the m;onkey

Every monkey needs a leader.

Not a dictator.
Not a coach.
Not a motivational YouTube video.

A **leader** -
someone who understands, guides, reassures, and supports.

That someone is **you**.

Not because you are perfect.
Not because you are wise.
Not because you have superhuman discipline.

You become the CEO because:

The monkey trusts YOU more than anyone else.

And trust is the first rule of leadership.

Let's break down what it means to become
the CEO of your inner monkey.

CEO Rule #1: You Don't Control the Monkey - You Guide It

Most people try to control their minds like a badly paid local security officer dealing with a riot.

They tighten the rules.
They pack the day with tight schedules.

They push themselves with constant inner pressure.
When that doesn't work, they upgrade to harsh self-talk, a little guilt, a little shame, a sprinkle of perfectionism, and a generous side dish of comparison and fear.

From outside, it looks like "discipline."
From inside it feels like living with a strict boss who never leaves your head - and somehow still expects the monkey to happily show up for work.

This doesn't work.

Because controlling a monkey is impossible.

Guiding a monkey is easy.

Guidance is emotional.
Control is mechanical.

Guidance says:
"I understand what you're feeling. Let's go together."

Control says:
"Why can't you just do it?"

One builds cooperation.
The other builds rebellion.

A real CEO knows the difference.

CEO Rule #2: Safety > Performance

Your monkey cannot perform if it doesn't feel safe.

Emotional safety is what your monkey needs before it even thinks about cooperating.

It's that feeling when the task in front of you looks like something a normal human can do today - not a heroic lifelong mission. The room is calm enough that your nervous system isn't scanning for danger. The stakes don't feel like, "If I mess this up, my entire life collapses."

A pressured monkey freezes.
A safe monkey moves.

Every time.

You need to tell the monkey that:

You're not secretly planning to punish yourself if it goes wrong.
You're not sprinting against an invisible clock.
You're not hearing an imaginary audience judging every move.
You're not demanding perfection - just an honest attempt.

In that space, the monkey doesn't feel hunted.
It feels invited.

This is why your night meetings work.
You created an inner environment
where the monkey feels partnered,
not threatened.

CEO Rule #3: Set Clear, Small, Non-Scary Goals

A CEO doesn't dump everything into the task list.

A CEO prioritizes.

Your monkey only needs:

- 1 big thing
- 2 medium things
- 3 small things

This is enough to shift a week,
a month,
a life.

Small goals don't demotivate.
Small goals **activate.**

The monkey feels:
"I can do this."

That one sentence
is more powerful than any motivational speech.

CEO Rule #4: Bananas Are Mandatory

You must reward your monkey.

Not as bribery,
but as **emotional nutrition**.

Bananas tell the monkey:

"You are not a slave. You matter."

When the monkey feels valued,
it shows up with energy
you didn't even know you had.

Most grown-ups run out of motivation
because they ran out of bananas.

A CEO who doesn't celebrate their team
loses their team.

A CEO who doesn't celebrate themselves
loses themselves.

CEO Rule #5: Manage the Energy, Not the Clock

This is a secret all great leaders know:

Time doesn't create productivity.
Energy does.

You can give the monkey 8 hours
and get nothing.

Or give it 30 minutes
and get brilliance.

Real energy doesn't come from coffee and motivational quotes.

It starts with emotional safety - that quiet inner sense that nothing terrible will happen if today is imperfect. It gets a huge boost from boring things like good sleep and basic clarity about what you're actually doing. It stays alive when you give yourself micro-breaks, a few well-placed bananas, and expectations that feel human instead of robotic.

Put that inside a reasonably calm environment, lower the invisible pressure a few notches, and something interesting happens:
you don't have to "force" performance anymore.

The monkey just gets up and works, almost like it was its own idea.

When you manage time forcefully,
the monkey panics.

But,

when you manage energy,
the monkey performs naturally.

CEO Rule #6: Speak Monkey Language

You now know the monkey's language. It is about raw feelings and impulses like fears, urges, boredom, joy, restlessness - scattered emotional waves.

A CEO listens.

A CEO responds in the correct language:

Not "Should."
Not "Must."
Not "Why are you like this?"
Not "Get your act together."

The CEO speaks gently:

"This feels heavy, right? Let's make it smaller. Let's take a quick break."
"Want a banana first?"
"Let's try again tomorrow. It's okay to fail."

You use intelligence to plan.
You use emotion to lead.

That balance is the superpower.

CEO Rule #7: Make Failure Non-Threatening

This rule changes everything.

When failure feels dangerous,
the monkey rebels.

When failure feels safe,
the monkey experiments, explores, tries, and grows.

A CEO knows:

Failure isn't an ending.
Failure is feedback.
Failure is discovery.
Failure is data.

And most importantly:

Failure is a normal part of being human.

When you stop punishing mistakes,
you stop fearing them.

When you stop fearing mistakes,
your growth becomes effortless.

The CEO Mindset in One Line

Here is the purest expression of this chapter, distilled into a single line:

m; note

You don't become the CEO by controlling the monkey.
You become the CEO when the monkey trusts you enough to follow.

That's the shift: from force to partnership,
from guilt to guidance, from rigid discipline to alignment, from pressure to emotional intelligence.

This is the leadership we were never taught.

But now you know.

In the next chapter,
you will learn how to create "The Exit Interview" -
a powerful closing ritual that releases emotional tension
and prepares your monkey for growth.

12 - the exit interview: releasing the monkey you used to be

Before a new chapter of life begins,
the old chapter must close.

This is not a meeting.
Not a plan.
Not a strategy.

This is a farewell.

A gentle conversation with the version of your monkey
that carried all your fears,
your shame,
your pressure,
your guilt,
your insecurities,
your old patterns,
and your old story.

The Night Meeting (Chapter 8)
helped you plan *tomorrow's* life.

The Exit Interview helps you release
the life that got you here.

One prepares.
The other frees.

Both are needed.

Because before transformation can begin,
something inside you must be allowed to end.

Why an Exit Interview Matters

Every major emotional shift begins with acknowledgement.

Not change.
Not discipline.
Not motivation.

Acknowledgement.

Because the monkey inside you carries the emotional memory
of **every version** you've ever been:

- the scared you
- the overwhelmed you
- the perfectionist you
- the insecure you
- the tired you

All of them leave fingerprints on your habits,
your expectations,
your reactions,
your fears.

An Exit Interview is how you finally say:

"Thank you for bringing me this far.
But I don't need to carry this weight anymore."

This is not a cleansing.
It is an honoring.

You are not deleting your past.
You are releasing your attachment to it.

How to Conduct the Exit Interview

This is a ritual of release, not responsibility.

Find a quiet moment.
Sit comfortably.
Let the shoulders soften, the breath deepen, the mind unclench.

Your monkey doesn't need intensity.
It needs gentleness.

Then ask it three questions -
slowly, softly, without judgment.

Question 1: "What hurt you the most?"

The monkey never forgets the wounds.
It stores it under procrastination, hesitation, irritability, perfectionism, avoidance and sometimes emotional shutdown.

All protective behaviors
are rooted in unspoken pain.

Let the monkey point to moments:

A childhood embarrassment.
A breakup.
A failure nobody knows about.
A job loss.
A harsh comment.
A moment of self-doubt.
A year that broke you.
A day that changed everything.

Let it speak without filters.

Sometimes, your adult self doesn't remember - but the monkey always does.

Naming pain begins healing.

Question 2: "What are you still carrying that wasn't yours to hold?"

This is the deep one.

The monkey often carries another person's expectations, criticism and standards. It often carries baggage of generational fear or school trauma or past labels or guilt you inherited.

Some of these weights are decades old.

Some were handed to you
before you even understood language.

Let the monkey reveal:

"I'm carrying pressure that wasn't mine."
"I'm carrying fear that didn't start with me."
"I'm carrying someone else's anger."
"I'm carrying a failure I never processed."
"I'm carrying the memory of being misunderstood."
"I'm carrying the fear of becoming small again."

When you let the monkey separate
what belongs to you
from *what was forced upon you...*

Something inside you untangles.

The emotional knot loosens.

The mind breathes.

Question 3: "What do you want me to change before we move forward?"

This is where the monkey becomes wise.

It might say:

"I need more rest."
"I need smaller goals."
"I need more play."
"I need gentler mornings."
"I need more joy."
"I need less comparison."

"I need space."
"I need you to stop hurting me with your expectations."

This last one strikes deeply.
Because it is often true.

Most of the monkey's wounds
come not from the world
but from the pressure we inflict on ourselves.

And acknowledging that
is the beginning of emotional maturity.

The Emotional Shift That Follows

Once the monkey has spoken,
once the truth has surfaced,
once the past has been honored...

A shift happens.

You feel the body soften.
The mind quietens.
The breath deepens.
The chest lightens.

The monkey feels:

- seen
- understood
- safe

- relieved
- respected
- ready

A monkey that has released the past
doesn't fear the future.

This is why the Exit Interview
is the final clearing
before the true transformation begins.

This is the end
before a new beginning.

A soft closing
before the powerful opening.

Here's the part nobody explained to you out loud:

m; note

Your old monkey was never wrong.
It was simply tired.

It deserves to retire with honor.

And tomorrow,
when you wake...

You won't be meeting
the same monkey.

You'll be meeting
the one that trusts you.

The one you freed.

The one ready to walk with you
into the next chapter of your life.

The CEO version of you
cannot rise
until the old monkey version of you
is allowed to rest.

Let it rest.

And then rise.

final ceo speech -
"the day you finally gave ***********"

Sit with me for a moment.

No rush.
No pressure.
No pretending.

You've walked a long path through this book - through honesty, laughter, memories, mistakes, through chaos, through truth, through the soft corners of your past.

And now...
everything inside you becomes quiet.

The monkey is calm.
Your breath is steady.
Your chest feels lighter,
as if something invisible finally loosened its grip.

This is the moment where you stop reading as a reader
and begin listening as the **leader of your inner world.**

So take a breath.

Let the world slow.
Let your shoulders drop.
Let your monkey settle.

Something important is about to happen.

This is the day you finally gave _____.

I'm not filling that blank for you yet.

Because the truth that belongs there
is not a word you understand with your mind.
It's a truth you recognize with your heart.

You've spent years feeding yourself deadlines, criticism, discipline, expectations, pressure, logic, explanations, comparisons - and long stretches of silent disappointment.

But none of those ever helped.

Because none of those ever reached
the small emotional creature inside you
that has been trying to follow your commands
without ever being understood.

You thought you needed control.
You thought you needed discipline.
You thought you needed toughness.

But the monkey needed something else entirely.

And deep inside you...
you already know what that blank is whispering.

Not yet.
Hold it.
Feel the tension build.

Let's go deeper.

All your life, you believed life was a fight against yourself.
A battle between two halves of your mind.

A thinker.
A feeler.
A human.
A monkey.

You assumed this duality meant you were broken,
conflicted,
inconsistent,
undisciplined.

But here's the secret I saved for this exact moment
-
a quiet truth most people will overlook,
but the attentive ones will sense:

You were never meant to be one.
You were designed to be two.

A mind that feels.
A mind that leads.

And the breakage in your life
never came from duality.

It came from **denying** one-half of yourself
while overworking the other.

That's the wound.
That's the reason.
That's the missing piece.

And it brings us back to the blank.

Are you ready?

Here is the truth, the entire book has been waiting to tell you.

m; note

"People don't fail because they're weak.
They fail because they never permitted themselves to be who they truly are."

There it is.
The missing word.
The missing truth.
The missing key you've been chasing for years.

Permission.

Permission to feel.
Permission to rest.
Permission to play.
Permission to slow down.
Permission to be emotional.

Permission to be human.
Permission to be imperfect.
Permission to fall and rise again.
Permission to lead gently.
Permission to stop performing.
Permission to exist without apology.

Permission.

The one thing you never gave.
The one thing the monkey always needed.
The one truth that transforms everything.

m; social oath

Optional.
But secretly powerful.

If you want to lock this in, don't just think it. Put a tiny footprint of this moment outside your head. At some point in the next 24 hours, share a one-line promise to your monkey somewhere outside this book - WhatsApp status, Instagram story, LinkedIn Post, Facebook, X (Twitter), anywhere you feel safe. It can be anonymous. It can be tiny. It can be private to your close friends list.

You can borrow this line if you like:

"**m;** I'm done chasing perfection. I'm building a life where my inner monkey feels safe, welcomed, and fully permitted to be weird - as long as we walk forward together. **#InnerMonkey #mproject**"

If you're allergic to public posts, just write that line in your notebook with a small m; beside it. The oath still counts.

m; reminder
For all ready to use worksheets, templates, and a small surprise
see "Monkey Lab - Resources" at the end of this book.

When permission enters the heart,
resistance dissolves.
Chaos softens.
The monkey exhales.
And your life - finally - starts to feel livable.

And now... the circle closes.

What began as a story about struggle
ends as a story about softness.

What began with duality
ends with unity.

What began with chaos
ends with leadership.

What began with pressure
ends with permission.

This is the moment the old you
meets the new you.

This is the handover ceremony
between who you were
and who you will become.

And tomorrow morning, when you wake,
you will not wake as the person who started this book.

You will wake as someone who finally understands
that gentleness is not weakness -
it is intelligence in its highest emotional form.

Real leadership begins where self-violence ends.

Close your eyes for a second.

And whisper softly to your monkey:

"I give you permission."

Because the moment you say that...

Your monkey relaxes.
Your mind clears.
Your emotions align.
Your energy returns.
Your resistance melts.
Your life changes direction.

This is the day you finally gave ______.

And now you know
what belonged in that blank all along.

One last thing.

There is a deeper truth inside you -
a truth we have not opened yet,
a truth tied to that mysterious duality.
I mentioned it only once.

Most people will forget it, or assume it was poetic noise.

But you won't.

You will feel that it was a clue.
A door.
A seed waiting quietly in the soil.

And one day,
when the next book arrives,
you will look back at this page
and whisper:

"It was planned from the beginning."

Because it was.

Close the book gently.
Place your right hand on your heart.
And tell your monkey:

"We got this."

And you do.
You really, truly do.

Your monkey knows it,

already.

m;onkey lab
- resources

You made it to the end of the book.
You've met your monkey, argued with it, fed it, and maybe even forgave it a little.

This section keeps all the practical tools in one place,
so you don't have to chase links or QR codes while you're in the middle of a sentence.

Everything here lives in **one single page online**:

Scan the QR code or visit: **ullasdas.com/inner-monkey**

That one link gives you access to:

- The **CEO Playbook** – printable daily pages.
- The **Social Kit** – shareable posts, captions & a one-page summary.
- **Surprise free gift** - a reward for your inner monkey.

Everything here is optional.
The real work is still the quiet conversation between you and your inner monkey.

1. The CEO Playbook - Your Monkey-Friendly Planner

This is a **printable mini-planner** built for normal, messy humans.

Inside the Playbook you'll find:

- A **Night Meeting page**
  to review your day with your monkey, honestly.
- A **1–2–3 Daily Plan**
  (1 big thing, 2 medium things, 3 tiny things your monkey can accept).
- A simple **"How did my monkey feel today?"** tracker
  so you can notice patterns without turning it into a full-time job.

You'll see a download button for the Playbook

on the Resources page after you scan the QR or open the link provided above.

Start small: use it for just **three nights - night review + next-day plan, and a quick morning check-in.**

If your monkey likes it, keep going.
If it doesn't, change the page instead of blaming yourself.

2. Social Kit - Share Your Monkey Story

If you like posting online or simply want an easy way to tell a friend about this book, the Social Kit is for you.

Inside you'll find:

- **Quote cards** from the book,
  already sized for stories and posts.
- Short **caption starters**
  you can copy, paste, and edit in your own voice.
- A one-page **summary of the idea**
  you can send to someone whose monkey is tired.

The same QR code and link take you there – super easy.

Use these as prompts, not rules.
Your story, your monkey, and your honesty
will always matter more than any template.

If you never print a single page
or download a single file,
this book has still done its job

if you treat your inner monkey
a little more kindly
than before you opened it.

Tools are optional.
Your relationship with your mind is not.

Thank you for reading, for trying,
and for staying in the room
with your monkey.

About the Author

Ullas Das works in technology as an Agile delivery leader and AI enthusiast, helping teams ship complex products without burning out.

Earlier in his life, he wrote Bengali stories for magazines such as Sananda, Unish Kuri, and Anandamela, and later for audio and video on YouTube. His Bengali storytelling channels now have over 150,000 subscribers, and one of them has received the YouTube Silver Play Button.

Ullas is also the founder of 24by7Publishing.com in India, a self-publishing platform that has helped thousands of independent authors act as the CEO *of their own books* – keeping control over their rights, creative choices, and global reach instead of waiting for permission from traditional publishers. He has written and published several books on AI, Agile project management, and fiction.

Be the CEO of Your Inner Monkey brings together his experience in projects, storytelling, and AI to offer a kinder way to lead your own mind. You can find more at ullasdas.com.

www.ingramcontent.com/pod-product-compliance
Lightning Source LLC
Chambersburg PA
CBHW011802160726
48282CB00035B/1238